inkblots

For Elementary Creative Writing

K-3

by
Pat Watson and Janet Watson

Editor: Cherisse Mastry
Page Layout & Graphics: Cherisse Mastry & Kirstin Simpson
Cover/Book Design: Educational Media Services

These popular series of books are available from ECS Learning Systems, Inc.

The Once Upon a Time Series™	Gr. K-2	10 Titles
The Math Whiz Kids™	Gr. 3-5	4 Titles
The Little Red Writing Book	Ages 6-12	3 Titles
The Bright Blue Thinking Book	Ages 6-12	3 Titles
Writing Warm-Ups™	Gr. K-6	2 Titles
Foundations for Writing	Gr. 2-8	2 Titles
Springboards for Reading	Gr. 3-6	1 Title
The Picture Book Companion	Gr. K-3	3 Titles
Novel Extenders	Gr. 1-6	7 Titles
Quick Thinking™	Gr. K-12	2 Titles
Thematic Units	Gr. K-8	23 Titles
Activity Books	Gr. K-12	11 Titles
EnviroLearn™	Gr. K-5	5 Titles
Home Study Collection™ (Basic Skills & More)	Gr. 1-6	18 Titles
Test Preparation Guides	Gr. 2-12	41 Titles
Booklinks	Gr. 3-8	1 Title

To order, contact your local school supply store or write for a complete catalog:

ECS Learning Systems, Inc.
P.O. Box 791439
San Antonio, Texas 78279-1439

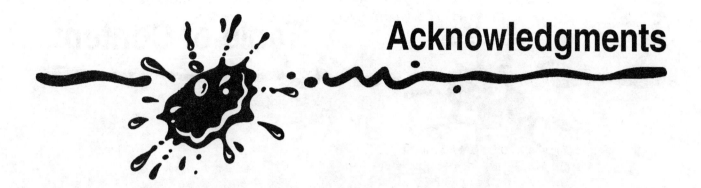

Acknowledgments

Thanks to Kimberly Keller, art teacher, Georgetown ISD (Georgetown, TX) for contributing to the section, Writing Stages (p. 16).

Thanks to Pat Benson, retired science teacher, Muleshoe ISD (Muleshoe, TX) and Temple ISD (Temple, TX) for the suggested grading criteria used for monitoring peer response groups (p. 32). She now resides in College Station, Texas.

Thanks to Cindy Grohman, teacher at Carver Elementary School, Georgetown ISD (Georgetown, TX) for allowing us to use the assignment form (p. 102).

Thanks to our students, who inspired us to develop creative ideas to challenge their thinking and writing skills.

Table of Contents

Preface

Getting Started   9
    Modifications for K-1   10
    Word Lists   13
    Activities   14
    Writing Stages   16

Journaling and Letter Writing   21
    Overview   22
    Journal Ideas for K-1   24
    Journal Ideas for 2-3   25
    Letter Writing   27

Developing a Writing Program   29
    Directives   30
    Peer Response Groups
        Grades K-1   31
        Grades 2-3   32

Writing Assignments   35
    Types of Writing   36
    Descriptive Writing   38
    Narrative Writing   42
    Expository Writing   44
    Persuasive Writing   46

A Closer Look at Stories   49
    Foreword   50
    Story Writing   52
    Autobiographical Writing   58
    Characterizations   60

A Closer Look at Poetry   63
    Poetry Writing   64
    Poetry Notebook   66

Reading and Writing Connection   71
    Assignments   72
       Grades K-1   73
       Grades 2-3   76
       Books to Read Aloud   80
       Additional Assignments   82
       Book Report and Story Summary Ideas   83

Short Assignments   85
    Word Studies   86
       Additional Short Assignments   88

Student Handouts   91

Student Work   101

About the Authors   111

Preface

Most children have an innate love of words they hear and speak. The goal of elementary creative writing is to capitalize on this love of words and to guide students as they learn to express themselves creatively. The exercises and assignments in *Inkblots for Elementary Creative Writing* are designed to help students express their perceptions as they hear, feel, touch, see, think, and wonder.

This syllabus for grades K-3 is divided into 10 sections: Getting Started, Journaling and Letter Writing, Developing a Writing Program, Writing Assignments, A Closer Look at Stories, A Closer Look at Poetry, Reading and Writing Connection, Short Assignments, Student Handouts, and Student Work. Assignments for this age student include writing sentences, paragraphs, letters, stories, advertisements, and poems. The Getting Started section includes guidelines to help the teacher understand the stages of writing from "scribbling" to accomplished writing.

Each section is designed to guide teachers to help students think and write creatively. Unit plans in the Writing Assignments section state an objective, focus activity, process for teaching, and assignment. In addition, several lessons include activities and assignment extensions. The Reading and Writing Connection section lists a wide variety of children's books, each with a brief synopsis and accompanying writing assignment.

Teacher participation is a vital part of any creative writing program. Learn to write with your students and to enjoy what they have written. As teachers enthusiastically share their own ideas, students come to recognize learning as a never-ending process and writing as a delight.

The material in this book has evolved over many years of teaching creative writing. We hope the ideas in this syllabus inspire you, the teacher, to have fun and to enjoy the "art" of teaching students creative writing.

Getting Started

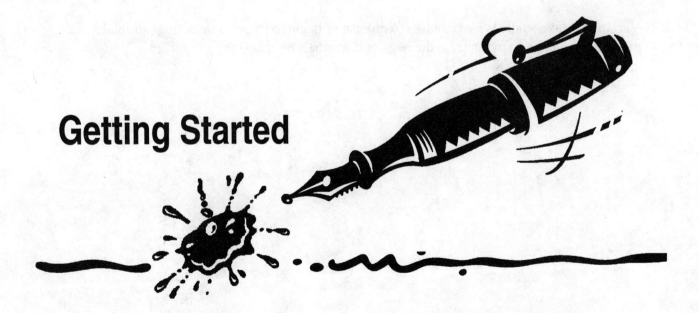

Modifications for K-1

For students in grades K-1, place emphasis on language development rather than writing. Very young children should not be rushed into writing; however, preparatory exercises help students associate the oral word with the written word. Modifications are included in topical sections of the book. Many of the adjustments are appropriate for students in grades 2-3 who are not yet up to grade level.

Group Activities

Group Stories promote transfer from oral to written communication. Students hear themselves speak the words and then see the words in print. Give a story starter, and have students make up a simple story; consider tape recording the story. Write the story on poster board.

Drama Day develops listening skills, teaches transference of words into actions, and strengthens sequencing skills. Invite an older student or an adult to read a story to the children. Assign parts and have students act out the story. Include everyone (sound effects, stage crew, prompter).

Puppet Theater: Get a large refrigerator box; cut a rectangular hole in the upper part to simulate a stage. Have students make puppets using construction paper and markers. Place the puppets on long sticks. Have the puppets appear from the rear of the box as the story is read. This activity works well with fairy tales.

Variation: Have students make masks (using paper bags) to wear while acting out their parts. They can paste pictures on the bags or draw their own designs.

Individual Activities

Picture Stories enhance sequencing skills. Placing pictures left to right prepares students to read left to right. This activity reinforces self-concept while the scrapbook project (Activity 2) stresses cohesiveness of a group.

1. Have students draw pictures to tell a story. Suggestions: "My House," "My Family," "My Pet," "A Visit with Grandparents," "Someday I'll Be," "Our Field Trip." Have them share their stories with the class. To simplify this assignment, fold a sheet of paper in fourths; unfold. The child then has four blocks in which to place the picture story.

2. Place students' pictures (students can use annual school photos) on separate sheets of paper. Teacher or aide writes a story as students relate two or three sentences about themselves to accompany their pictures. Make a class scrapbook.

3. Read a book to the children. Have them draw a picture that shows the funniest, most exciting, or saddest incident in the book. Have students explain their pictures to the class.

4. Make a booklet with large pictures and accompanying text of a familiar rhyme such as "Brown Bear, Brown Bear, What Do You See?" Have students color the pictures and "read" along with the teacher. Repeat the same story periodically.

Dictated Stories teach students to associate pictures with words and allow them to hear their spoken words read from written form. Have each student dictate a story to teacher, aide, or parent (via homework instructions). Students illustrate and tell their stories to the class. Read their stories aloud to the class.

Storytelling Days reinforce development of language skills. Have each student tell a story to the class.

Suggestions:

1. Give each student a picture. Have students tell a story that relates to their picture.

2. Have each student draw a picture and tell a story about the picture.

3. Students can tell a familiar story in their own words.

4. Have students place three or four pictures in correct order, then tell a story to fit the pictures. Teacher or aide can copy the story as the child narrates.

Copying develops reading/writing readiness through the hearing/seeing/writing of letters and words. Begin by having children trace or copy single letters (place the letter on a page with a picture of an object that starts with that letter). Expand the activity to include words. Have students copy the same material at the same time as the words are read.

Word Lists

The activities in this and the following three sections can be used as springboards for creative writing assignments. Suggested assignments are included when applicable.

Creating word lists should be a class project. Add to the lists as students discover other words. These lists will be useful for various writing assignments. The words can be placed on poster board for use throughout the year, or older students can make their own lists and keep them in a notebook. The length of the lists will depend on the students' grade level.

Spelling words: List the correct spelling for commonly used words. Grades K-1: Begin with simple words; place on poster board with accompanying picture.

Color words: List the correct spelling for common colors; add synonyms for colors; add unusual colors.

Shape words: List shape words, such as circle, square, triangle, rectangle, and others as needed.

Sound words: List sound words that are nouns (bells, sirens) and adjectives (clanging, shouting).

Words to describe people: Compile words used to describe people. Use common words, such as short and tall, blond and brunette; add others as needed (friendly, shy, outgoing, considerate).

Emotion words: List words that stir emotions. Use common words, such as happiness and anger; add others as needed (sympathy, disappointment, anxiety, revenge).

Category words: Create a list of words that describe a category: musical instruments, modes of transportation, occupations, foods, toys, tools, feelings, buildings, furniture, sports activities, age groups (children, teenagers, adults), topics (family, school).

Lazy words: List words that are overused and make writing dull. For example, include nouns (girl, boy), adjectives (good, bad, big, little, pretty, best), adverbs (very, really, too), and verbs (got, love, ran).

Dynamic words: List unusual words, similes, metaphors, vivid descriptive words, and strong action verbs.

Connecting words: List words that connect compound or compound/complex sentences (because, if, however, therefore, so, when, while, but, and, although, since) or words that introduce an idea (first, last, second) and connect paragraphs.

Variation: Homonym, synonym, and antonym lists can be created as an alternative activity or assignment.

Activities

Idea Boxes

To create idea boxes, mount material on index cards; create card files for the following short assignments.

Headlines can be a class project for younger students or an individual project for older students. Have students choose an unusual headline and create a story that fits the headline. Read some of the students' stories aloud, then read the original article and compare. File original stories.

> **Grades K-1**: Choose a simple headline; guide the students as they make up a story. Read their story aloud and have students draw a picture to illustrate.

Advertisements: Select an advertisement with colorful pictures. Cut away the message, and have students create an original advertisement, either as a class project or individually.

> **Grades K-1**: Using colorful advertisements for toys or other simple objects, have students brainstorm words that describe the object. Let them relate orally why they would or would not want this object.

©ECS Learning Systems, Inc., San Antonio, Texas

Picture Files

1. Collect pictures from magazines, mount them on heavy paper, and laminate them.

2. Write questions on the back of each picture to stimulate creative thinking.

3. Include photos of people showing a variety of emotions (babies' expressions lead to wonderful, creative ideas), animals in natural and unusual habitats, insects, landscapes, foods, occupations, household items, unusual objects, weather (storm clouds, lightning).

Picture Files can encompass a wide variety of ideas. Form questions around why, what, how, where, sequence, predicted outcomes, realism/fantasy, etc.

Grades K-1: Use the pictures for discussion, and create a class story. Write the story on poster board for students to "read."

Grades 2-3: Students can write their own stories and read them to the class. Assignments can include descriptive, expository, narrative, or persuasive writing.

Writing Stages

Students come into our classrooms with a variety of backgrounds and skills. Through understanding the stages of writing development, teachers can identify specific needs of individual students and monitor writing improvement on an individual basis.

Stage One: Beginning Writing

- Scribbles randomly*
- Acts as if (s)he can read what has been written
- Scribbles with some sense of direction
- Forms letters
- Writes own name (often in all capital letters)
- Copies what someone has written
- Dictates words or short phrases (for objects, pictures, experiences)

Stage Two: Writing Words

- Writes family names (Mom, Dad)
- Shows some understanding of word length
- Understands spaces between words
- Is unconcerned with spelling and/or punctuation

Stage Three: New Words/Short Phrases

- Writes new words
- Completes pattern sentences with word or phrase: "I am...."; "That is a...."; "I like...."
- Writes short caption (two or three words) for picture
- Writes simple phrases

* Any scribbling is a step forward in the child's realization that marks on paper can be read; a communication value; a pre-writing sign.

Stage Four: Simple Sentences

- Composes sentences by following the pattern of a model sentence
- Writes simple, unrelated sentences

Stage Five: Combines Sentences into Simple Paragraph

- Organizes related sentences
- Writes short paragraph on one subject
- Spells phonetically but somewhat consistently
- Writes short letters, such as thank-you notes

Stage Six: Beginning Story Writing

- Composes short narrative with simple sentences
- Uses many combining words, such as "and" or "but"
- Shows inconsistent capitalization and punctuation
- Uses standard spelling for some words

Stage Seven: Expanded Story Writing

- Writes stronger sentences with fewer connecting words
- Writes longer stories
- Uses more descriptions, especially colors
- Composes stories with a beginning, a middle, and an end
- Expands sentence writing to include compound and/or complex sentences
- Improves capitalization skills
- Uses more correct end punctuation

Stage Eight: Progressive Writing Skills

- Expands sentence patterns to include stronger adjectives, adverbs, phrases (prepositional, adverbial)
- Expands ability to use mechanics correctly to include initial capitalization and end punctuation, commas in a series, quotation marks for dialogue, and more correct spelling
- Uses correct paragraph structure: topic sentence, 3 details, concluding sentence
- Writes descriptive, expository, narrative, and persuasive paragraphs
- Edits own work for: overuse of "lazy" words, content, sentence structure (run-ons, fragments), paragraph structure, transitions (first, last)

Stage Nine: Advanced Writing Skills

- Combines two or more paragraphs with appropriate transitions
- Writes stronger introduction and conclusion
- Understands and uses literary devices: simile, metaphor, exaggeration, alliteration
- Expands story writing to show understanding of plot, conflict, suspense, setting, and characterization
- Expands self-editing skills to include: punctuation, spelling, grammar, tense, and voice
- Writes to inform: expository essays, book reports, news articles, letters
- Writes to express self and entertain others: short stories, poetry, drama, diaries
- Writing demonstrates understanding of cause/effect, problem solving, sequencing, comparison/contrast, summaries, generalization, and types of narration
- Writes research paper demonstrating ability to develop and use bibliography, take notes, outline, and use parenthetical citations

For student writing samples with corresponding writing assignment, refer to Student Work 1, pp. 102-104.

notes

Journaling and
Letter Writing

21

The road to becoming a good writer is paved by simply writing. A teacher's goal is to help students master writing skills painlessly. Journaling is a wonderful start. By keeping a journal, children can grow in expression and communication, as well as discover some surprising things about themselves through writing.

The most successful way to approach journaling is simply to expect students to write daily. Students keep their journals in a notebook. Upon entering the classroom each day, they find an assignment on the board. This routine proves to be a wonderful management technique. By adhering to this schedule, the teacher eliminates much potentially wasted time. The students enter the classroom, put things away, sharpen their pencils, and quickly get to work on their daily journals.

Evaluation of journal work is left to the discretion of the teacher. Allow mistakes and much freedom as students explore writing through this avenue. Expect more fine-tuned products from assignments completed in the other content areas.

Grade on participation. A check or comment at the top of each entry shows you actually read their efforts and provides a positive incentive for students. If a student feels an entry is too personal for even the teacher to read, (s)he places a paper clip on the top of the page. Check only to see that the assignment has been completed.

Children often formulate their ideas for stories and journal entries from home experiences. Be careful not to analyze children's backgrounds from either their stories or their journal entries. Children have vivid imaginations; accept their writing as products of that imagination.

Parental questions regarding privacy issues in journal writing occasionally surface. Teachers may also have concerns regarding this matter. If you feel uneasy about privacy issues, monitor your journal prompts carefully. Journal writing is meant to allow children to experience the pure joy and freedom of writing. A wide variety of ideas leads to "fun" writing and does not intrude upon a child's privacy.

Incorporate as many other content areas as possible into daily journal writing. Have beginning students draw pictures in response to a prompt and add a word or two of explanation. Have them progress from a few words to a sentence or two. Eventually, you can expect students to write from a few sentences to two paragraphs, although some students may write more. Third-grade students can often write at least one page per entry.

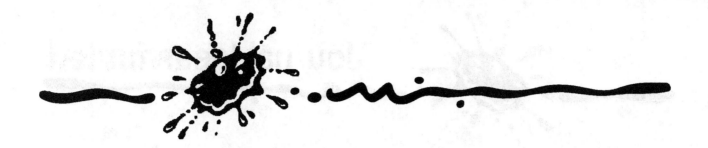

Beginning Journal Entries

With beginning writers, emphasize what students *can do*, not what they can't do. Young children can express, in some way, what they are feeling.

Provide paper and crayons for the children. Let them draw pictures and ask them to label parts of their pictures. Prepare booklets for younger children to use as journals. Each page should contain a message for the day, leaving space for children to write one or two words (e.g., "Today I feel...."). Children can then illustrate the message. Depending on their experience and ability, some first-grade students should be expected to write words and even sentences at the beginning of the year.

Journal Ideas for K-1

Beginning of School

1. Draw a picture of your favorite summer activity.

2. Draw a picture of yourself at the pool in your swimsuit.

3. Draw a picture of your two favorite animals at the zoo.

4. Draw two pictures, one as you arrive at the zoo, and one at the end of your visit (sequencing skills).

5. Draw a picture of yourself during the Fourth of July fireworks display. Were you excited, afraid, or both?

6. Draw a picture of a special adventure you shared with a grandparent or friend this summer.

Special Holidays

1. Draw a picture of your costume for the Harvest/Halloween Festival.

2. Draw five things you are thankful for or happy to have this Thanksgiving.

3. Write one sentence explaining why your favorite holiday is the best.

4. If you could pick an animal to enter in a contest at the county fair, which animal would it be? Draw a picture of your animal and you. Write a sentence or two explaining why your animal should win.

5. Draw pictures of your favorite things to do during the winter/Christmas holiday and tell why they are special to you (e.g., baking cookies, making ornaments, cooking, wrapping gifts, shopping). Share these pictures with the class.

 ©ECS Learning Systems, Inc., San Antonio, Texas

Journal Ideas for 2-3

Beginning of School

1. Describe your summer vacation in a few sentences.

2. Write about an adventure or experience you shared with a grandparent or relative this summer.

3. If you attended camp(s) this summer, write about some experiences you had.

4. Describe a normal summer day for you.

5. Describe your Fourth of July. Were you nervous or excited about the fireworks?

6. Choose a favorite book you read or had read to you recently, and tell about it in your own words.

7. Recall a movie you saw recently, and retell the ending.

8. Write two sentences describing how you felt the morning you walked into your new class.

9. Write two sentences describing your goals for this school year.

10. What is your favorite part of school so far? What is your least favorite part of school so far?

11. If you could give three suggestions to your principal to improve this school, what would they be?

12. If you were in charge of picking out a new school name and mascot, what would you choose and why?

13. How do you most enjoy spending your weekends?

Special Holidays and Events

1. Describe how you will dress for the Harvest/Halloween Festival.

2. Have you ever been really scared? Describe this experience.

3. If you could enter an animal in a contest at the county fair, what animal would you enter? Why should it win?

4. List five things you are thankful for this Thanksgiving season.

5. How does your family celebrate Thanksgiving?

Letter Writing

Students in kindergarten can draw pictures with an accompanying word or two. They can fill in one-word blanks on a prewritten note, or dictate a letter to the teacher or aide. Capitalize on students' desire to write notes to other students by establishing a "mail box" center with a container for each student. Occasionally, allow students a few minutes (possibly after lunch or recess) to write and deliver their notes. This and the following activities give students the practice they need to improve their letter-writing skills.

Have students:

1. Write thank-you letters to parents who assisted with class parties or other school events.

2. Write invitations to parents for school events.

3. Write letters to grandparents explaining what they want for Christmas. (For students who do not celebrate Christmas, write a letter to parent(s), describing a specific toy or gift and explaining why they want that particular item.)

4. Write a letter of appreciation to the principal for a special assembly or privilege. This can be a letter requesting a special event.

5. Write a letter of appreciation to the music or art teacher for a special presentation or display.

6. Write a note of appreciation to the custodian, bus driver, or school crossing guard.

7. Write a special letter to grandparents or an aunt or uncle on Valentine's Day.

8. Write a fan letter to a favorite musician or actor.

9. Join or start a pen pal program, either with students in another city or with students at another school in the same city.

10. Write letters to themselves. At the beginning of the school year, students list their desired accomplishments for the upcoming semester. During January, students list their New Year's resolutions. (Keep the letters in an envelope, and return them to the students at the end of the year.)

11. Write a letter to a favorite pet.

Developing a
Writing Program

Directives

1. Children learn to write by writing. Make assignments interesting, purposeful, and meaningful. Rather than focusing on exercises about "how to write," teach children to write what they see and feel. Consider developing individual spelling lists based on misspelled words in a student's writing.

2. Writing is a developmental process. For beginning writers, concentrate primarily on content. Children cannot learn to express themselves and master mechanics simultaneously.

3. Respond to the content with positive comments. Don't return a paper that is "bleeding to death." Nothing stifles early writing endeavors as much as a teacher's disapproval.

4. Gradually focus on mechanics and form. For example, concentrate on one or two areas of mechanics in a specific assignment. Give instructions before students begin the assignment, then give two grades: one for content and one for mechanics.

5. Accept children at their individual developmental levels. Read and comment on each student's paper accordingly. Set up student/teacher conferences that will enable you to offer suggestions and encouragement. In addition, have students plan a student/parent conference. Each student plans and conducts the conference. Students explain to parents the format and requirements for their sample writing assignments. Have parent(s) sign a conference sheet for their student's folder stating that their child has clearly explained the writing process.

6. Consider establishing peer response groups. Suggestions for establishing and monitoring these groups can be found on the following pages.

7. Allow students to write occasionally just for the fun of writing. This can be accomplished through journaling or letter writing.

8. Display students' papers in various stages of the process (brainstorming, rough draft), as well as finished products. Include sample work from all students, not just the neat, correct papers.

Peer Response Groups

Grades K-1

In small groups, discuss each child's work, have children show pictures and explain their writing, and read student-dictated stories. Allow students to comment on each other's stories, always stressing the need to be positive. As students comment, fill out an evaluation form (Student Handout 1, p. 92), for each child's folder.

Points to consider before having students work in peer response groups:

1. Students must always list at least one strength.

2. Students will respond to no more than one or two skills at a time. The scope of skills depends on grade level.

3. Change the response form to indicate the selected skill(s) and the specific target areas (e.g., clear beginning, middle, ending; punctuation; spelling; capitalization; sentence structure; overuse of "lazy" words).

Suggested target areas for peer comments:

1. Tell what you liked best about the paper.

2. List specific nouns, verbs, adjectives, and adverbs.

3. Was anything about the story unclear to you?

4. Summarize the story in one sentence.

5. Rewrite unclear sentences.

Grades 2-3

1. Assign students to groups of three or four students. Choose students with different personality types: the "leader," the "talker," the "quiet one." Keep the same groups for several assignments, unless the students have obvious difficulty working together.

2. Appoint a different group leader each time the group works together. Choose the leader based on objective criteria, such as the student with the closest birth date, or the student wearing a specific color.

3. Give a group grade. Suggested criteria for group grade (see note below):

   A. Each group starts the activity with 100 points.

   B. Deduct 10 points for each infraction of the following rules.

   • Only the leader may ask the teacher a question.

   • Students must remain on task (no visiting).

   • Discussion should be confined to within their own group.

   • Students should refrain from arguing.

An easy method for keeping track of a group's score is to use numbered cups containing 10 popsicle sticks or strips of paper. Number cups to correspond with groups. Remove one stick or strip from the group's cup each time an infraction of the rules occurs.

Note: A standard policy for group interaction creates a workable group atmosphere and employs "peer pressure" to encourage participating students to conform to the guidelines. As a result, students learn to work together and to depend on each other, rather than on the teacher.

4. Format:

    A. Before beginning group work, suggest that student authors list areas where they want a group response (e.g., content or sentence structure).

    B. Distribute evaluation sheets (Student Handout 2, p. 93). This form can also be used for teacher evaluation.

    C. Direct students to take turns reading papers aloud to the group; group members may offer positive comments.

    D. Have each student read the papers; write specific comments regarding content, clarity, and mechanics; and complete their evaluation sheets. Remind students that general comments such as "I liked it" will not help the author.

    E. Return papers to authors for question/answer session.

    F. Take up papers and make comments.

    G. Have students rewrite papers.

notes

Writing
Assignments

Types of Writing

The first part of this section explains different types of writing: descriptive, narrative, expository, persuasive. The second part includes classroom activities and assignments.

Descriptive Writing

Descriptive writing describes something clearly for the reader. The mental picture created may be of a person, place, thing, event, or experience. Descriptive writing allows the reader to see, hear, feel, taste, and/or smell what the author is describing. Often, this is only part of a longer piece of writing.

Teach students to describe the main object of a picture from top to bottom or from left to right and to describe the other parts last. In beginning writing exercises, number and label each part in correct order and have students write the description in that pattern. Stress that all writing must have a beginning and an ending; for example, begin with "This picture shows…." and end with "This is an unusual picture."

Narrative Writing

Narrative writing speaks to the reader, telling a story through a series of events. The events are usually arranged in chronological order. This account may be real or imaginary and may range from a short, simple narrative to a longer story. The author should use descriptive detail to explain the material.

Most children enjoy storytelling about real or imaginary events. The teacher's task is to guide them as they learn to put these stories on paper. Begin with a few sentences, which the student can dictate to the teacher or write with parental help at home.

 ©ECS Learning Systems, Inc., San Antonio, Texas

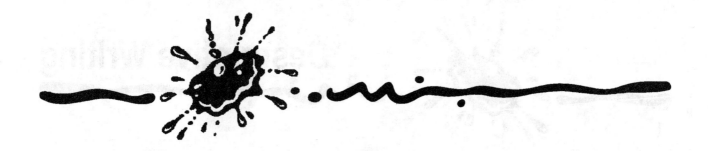

Expository Writing

Expository writing gives information or explains facts and ideas. This type of writing explains how to do something, what something means, why it is important, how it works, and/or when and where it occurs. Expository writing also includes comparison/contrast writing.

Persuasive Writing

Persuasive writing attempts to persuade the reader to believe an opinion. A good persuasive paper includes convincing reasons to support the author's opinion. Advertisements and editorials are good examples of persuasive writing.

Suggestions for all types of writing:

Grades K-1: Students and teacher brainstorm and develop ideas together; teacher writes or students complete work at home with parental assistance.

Grades 2-3: Demonstrate a variety of brainstorming ideas (outlining, mapping, clustering, webbing, story mapping, listing)*; students write sentences, paragraphs, or stories. Length and degree of difficulty should depend on grade level.

* Patterns included on pages 52-53.

Descriptive Writing

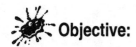

Objective:

• To demonstrate an understanding of descriptive writing by writing a paragraph (or short story) that appeals to the five senses

Focus Activity:

Discuss sensory experiences with students. Have students describe things they have tasted, smelled, seen, touched, or heard throughout the day. Together, develop lists of tasting, smelling, seeing, touching, and hearing words. Display lists for reference.

Process:

Discuss descriptive writing. Show students a picture and read a descriptive paragraph about it. Point out the importance of describing things in a set pattern (e.g., top to bottom; left to right). Select a common experience (e.g., lunch time) and develop a classroom paragraph.

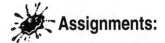 **Assignments:**

Grades K-1

1. Students dictate to the teacher one or two descriptive sentences about a picture or a personal experience; students illustrate. This can also be a homework assignment to be completed with parental assistance.

2. Students describe and draw a picture of their school building.

3. Students draw a picture of and write a descriptive sentence about their pet.

4. Students draw a picture of and write a descriptive sentence about their favorite toy.

Grades 2-3

1. Students write a paragraph that helps the reader smell and taste a favorite meal, see an unusual person, hear the sounds of the playground at recess, or feel the bark of a tree or other object. Illustrate. The degree of difficulty and length of descriptive writing depend on grade level.

2. Students write a description of the school (building, people). Illustrate.

3. Students write a descriptive paragraph about their pet. Illustrate.

4. Combine descriptive and narrative writing. Students write a descriptive paragraph about their hobby. Describe the required equipment, list places where they work on their hobby, and tell why it is a favorite. Allow students to bring a sample of their hobby or collection to show to the class. Have students read the paragraph describing their hobby/collection.

Extensions:

Grades K-1

1. Brainstorm and write on the board ideas for words that describe the sights, sounds, tastes, smells, and feelings of a day at the county or state fair. After brainstorming, students dictate, teacher writes.

2. Distribute pictures of a variety of animals to students and have them write a description of their picture. Display pictures and students dictate descriptions.

Grade 2

1. Students describe their neighborhood.

Grade 3

1. Students describe their neighborhood, telling what is pleasing and/or unpleasant to them. Include physical characteristics, types of people, and descriptions of houses, landscapes, and vehicles.

2. Students look through magazines and list ten descriptive words. Students exchange lists with a partner and write a story using words from partner's list.

3. Place several objects in small paper bags. Give one bag to each student. Tell students to leave the object in the bag and observe secretly and silently. Students write a description of their object and read it to the class; have other students draw the object as they visualize it. Suggested objects: feather, peanut, seashell, hair bow, shoelace, baby rattle, teething ring, eyelash curler, round hair brush, baby fork, cocoon, rubber band, button, toothpick, screw, tube of lip balm, battery.

©ECS Learning Systems, Inc., San Antonio, Texas

Grades K-3*

1. Students take an imaginary walk and write what they hear, see, smell, and touch. Illustrate.

2. Brainstorm and write on the board ideas for words that describe the sights, sounds, tastes, smells, and feelings of a day at the county or state fair. Have students write experiences of a day at the fair, either as a class activity or individually. This activity works well for writing about holiday dinners, a visit to the circus or zoo, or any special experience.

3. Students explain how cotton candy feels, smells, and tastes.

4. Students explain the taste, smell, and appearance of a hot dog to a visitor from outer space.

5. Distribute pictures of a variety of animals to students and have them write a description of their picture. Display pictures around the room. Take up and redistribute descriptive papers. Students match descriptive papers to pictures.

* For grades K-1, modify activities and use as class projects.

Narrative Writing

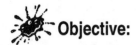

Objective:

• To write a selection which demonstrates an understanding of narrative writing style

Focus Activity:

Have students share an experience, such as a trip to the doctor, a visit to grandparents, or a birthday party.

Process:

Discuss narrative writing. Guide students to understand that narratives usually follow a sequential pattern. Select a recent experience in which the class participated. Outline steps that explain the experience.

Assignments:

Grades K-1: Students select a recent experience such as a trip or a visit (doctor, dentist, relatives). Students can either dictate narrative to the teacher or ask parents to help them write a brief narrative to hand in the following day. Be sure to send instructions home.

Grades 2-3: Students write a narrative about something that happened in their lives. Level of difficulty and length depend on grade level. (Stress using vivid words to convey the ideas and the importance of a strong beginning and ending.)

Extensions:

1. Students write a narrative about an imaginary trip they would like to take.

2. Students write a narrative about something interesting that has happened to them on the way to or from school. They can also make a map of the route from home to school.

3. Students select an entry from their journals and rewrite it as a narrative.

Expository Writing

 **Objective:**

• To demonstrate an understanding of expository writing by writing a step-by-step procedure

Focus Activity:

This focus activity requires prior planning. Show students a container with soil in it, then show them a plant growing in a container. Discuss how the plant might have gotten started in the soil.

Process:

Materials: small paper cups, soil, seeds, and a container of water. Instruct students on how to plant a few seeds in a cup. Demonstrate the procedure step-by-step as students follow along. Discuss the process.

©ECS Learning Systems, Inc., San Antonio, Texas

Assignments:

1. As a classroom activity or individually, students write about the process, from planting the seeds until the plant is full-grown.

2. Students write their own step-by-step procedure for something they know how to do.

Extensions:

1. Students write a step-by-step procedure for making something, such as a paper airplane.

2. Students prepare a sentence outline for the step-by-step events in "Jack and the Beanstalk," or another fairy tale or nursery rhyme.

3. Students draw a picture of their favorite game and explain how to play it.

4. Grades K-1: Students plan a trip to the zoo, draw pictures, and add as many words as they can.

5. Grades 2-3: Students plan a perfect party from beginning to end, giving the occasion, where it will be, who will be invited, what will be served, etc. This is a good collaborative assignment for small groups.

6. Grades 2-3: Students write the procedure for bathing a pet. The planning worksheet (Student Handout 3, p. 94) works well for this. Tell students to plan, then write.

Persuasive Writing

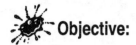 **Objective:**

• To write a selection which demonstrates an understanding of persuasive writing techniques

Focus Activities:

1. Display ads from magazines, especially those designed to appeal to children of the age group with which you are working. Ask students which products they would buy and why. Discuss current television advertisements that appeal to children.

2. Bring a toy that looked or sounded wonderful when it was advertised but broke the first time it was used. Ask students when they have had a similar experience. This is an excellent lesson on consumerism and is a useful tool for teaching discernment and smart shopping.

Process:

Discuss how print and television advertisements are designed to persuade the reader to buy a particular product. Point out persuasive words (biggest, best, etc.). Brainstorm and list words that are used in advertising directed at children.

©ECS Learning Systems, Inc., San Antonio, Texas

Assignments:

1. Show students a variety of products (pictures or actual objects) that are marketed for their age group. Develop an advertisement for one product (classroom activity or individually).

2. Remove the words from advertisements that feature vivid pictures. Distribute pictures to students; have them add persuasive words.

3. Brainstorm with students concerning a change they would like to see in the school. Write a classroom letter to the principal requesting the change. This is a positive way to demonstrate logical, reasonable methods of communication rather than impulsive, unreasonable methods.

notes

A Closer Look
at Stories

49

Foreword

Story writing is one of the core components of an elementary creative writing syllabus. Most students love listening to stories and have a wealth of ideas that can be developed into stories.

This unit includes a wide variety of suggestions for story writing. It also introduces a glossary of fundamental words. Together, these basic concepts will serve as a building block for more advanced writing. Use the glossary as needed for different grade levels. Some words may be too challenging for grades K-2. Focus on the concepts and not the words.

The assignments can be adapted for different grade levels. Younger students can write collaborative classroom stories. The expected length and level of difficulty can also be varied.

Glossary*

Protagonist: the main character

Antagonist: the character in opposition to the protagonist; can be another person, nature, or himself/herself

Point of View: first person narration (uses I, me, my, we, our, us); third person (uses he, she, they, them)

Setting: place and time period of story

Plot: sequence of events in story

Plot Structure:

1. Exposition: an introduction to the main characters, primary setting, and situations of the story
2. Rising Action: the events and complications that lead to an important dramatic point in the story
3. Climax: the point of greatest interest and emotional involvement in the story; turning point
4. Falling Action: the events that develop from the climax and lead to the conclusion
5. Denouement: the final outcome of the story; also called the resolution

Conflict: problem or struggle between protagonist and antagonist

Dialogue: conversation between two or more people

Foreshadowing: an event that hints at something that will happen later

Mood: emotional feeling of the story

* Teacher Reference

Story Writing

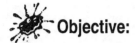 **Objective:**

• To help students develop their ideas into a logically organized story that incorporates descriptive and narrative writing

Focus Activities:

For each story-writing assignment, focus on the type of story you want the children to write.

1. Have students recall a favorite story from early childhood, tell why it was special, and list specific things they remember about the story.

2. Discuss types of stories (mystery, adventure, travel, fantasy).

Process:

Guide students in developing one or more types of planning designs. With grades K-1, start with the story map; at higher grade levels, other planning techniques can be introduced.

Outlining: Organize the subject matter into main topic and related subtopics.

Listing: Make a list of characters and events to organize ideas in a logical way.

Story Map: Draw a series of boxes (similar to a comic strip). In the first one, tell who the story is about and where and when it happened. In the other boxes, list events (or problems) in the story; in the last box, give the resolution of the story.

Variation: In a box on the upper left side, list who the story is about and where and when it happened. Draw a line to the right side and develop a vertical step-by-step box diagram in which you list events (or problems) in sequential order. Draw a line back to another box on the left in which you state the resolution of the story.

Clustering: Put the main idea in a center square. Draw circles branching out above and below the center to the left and right. Place subordinating ideas in these circles. This gives students a logical pattern to follow.

Webbing: Place a box containing the centralized concept (title) in the center of the page. Draw long lines branching out in four directions; place the main ideas on these lines. Draw smaller lines branching out from each long line; place the ideas connected to the main ideas on these lines.

Story Pyramid: Plan a story using a pyramid form.

```
                              1_____
                          2_____ _____
                      3_____ _____ _____
                  4_____ _____ _____ _____
              5_____ _____ _____ _____ _____
          6_____ _____ _____ _____ _____ _____
```

Directions: Students write the following on the lines indicated.

Line 1: Name of the main character

Line 2: Two words that describe the main character

Line 3: Three words that tell where and when the story takes place (setting)

Line 4: Four words that describe the setting

Line 5: Five words that tell the most important thing that happens (climax)

Line 6: Six words that tell how the story ends

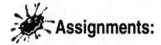**Assignments:**

This section includes a variety of ideas. Adapt the assignments for younger children by having students: write a class story together, draw pictures and add words according to their grade level, dictate their stories to a teacher, aide, or parent.

Story Starters

Travel Story

1. Plan a trip to see your grandparents. Tell how you will travel (car, plane, bus), what you will see on the way, and what you will do when you get there. Illustrate.

2. Imagine that you have been invited to Disneyland as a special guest of Mickey Mouse. Tell about your adventures. Illustrate.

3. Write a story beginning: "If I could take a trip anywhere in the world, I would go … because.…"

Fantasy Story

1. Pretend you are a tractor (bulldozer, crane, etc.). Write a story about your life. Illustrate.

2. Pretend you are a wild animal. Describe how you look and where you usually live. Tell how you act when roaming your own habitat, faced with danger, and/or placed in a zoo. Illustrate different parts of your story.

3. Write a story about a day in the life of … (feather, shoe, teething ring, rubber band, toothpick, cocoon, egg about to hatch, rhinoceros).

©ECS Learning Systems, Inc., San Antonio, Texas

4. Recall favorite fairy tales. (Discuss with the class patterns found in most fairy tales):

• Good overcomes evil by using magic
• Good vs. evil
• "Once upon a time...."
• "They lived happily ever after."

5. Write your own fairy tale.

Mystery Story

1. Write a story about "The Case of the Missing ... (Sneaker, Teacher, Class)."

2. Your teacher will read "Little Miss Muffet." Discuss Miss Muffet's reaction to the spider. Draw a picture of something you're afraid of and write a mystery story about the picture (who is afraid, why, what happens).

Adventure Story

Suggested Titles (Grades K-1, write together with teacher):

• The Lion Who Couldn't Roar
• The Giraffe Who Had a Sore Throat
• The Day the School Bus Ran Backward
• The Day I Bought Magic Shoes
• The Day I Became Invisible
• When I Was Captured by Pirates
• The Day My Mom (or Dad) and I Switched Places

Additional Story Ideas

1. Give each student an envelope containing 4 or 5 pictures. Have students put pictures in order and write a story relating to the pictures. This is a good sequencing exercise.

2. Take students on a nature hike around the school. Before the walk, tell students to look and listen carefully. After the walk, discuss sights and sounds. Write a story about the walk.

3. Tell students to think of a recent personal experience. On a sheet of paper, have students draw a "self portrait," with the face showing how they felt during the experience. Have students write a story to go with the picture.

4. Have students draw and cut out a hat that represents a career they want some day. Inside the design, have them write a story about that career.

5. Have students draw and cut out a vehicle and write a travel story; cut out a sports emblem (ball, bat, racket) and write a story about their favorite sport.

Collaborative Assignments

1. Place a variety of objects in a box. Gift wrap the box and place it on the teacher's desk or in another obvious place. Select a student (one with nearest birthday) to open the box and show the objects to the class. Write a class story about the objects (what they are, how they look, possible use).

2. Design an illustrated alphabet or number book. Each student can be responsible for one page. Bind the book and place it in the class library.

3. Plan a puppet show based either on a well-known story such as "The Three Bears" or on an original class story. Students design and make the puppets and write the script. Have a narrator, with students "acting" the parts. Cut out faces for puppets and place on sticks. Use a refrigerator box for your production. Cut the upper part out for the stage; open one side so students can enter and exit. Other large boxes can be used for the "wings" of the stage.

4. To incorporate descriptive and narrative writing: Choose a picture. On Day 1: Discuss; write a class descriptive paper about the picture. On Day 2: Choose one of the characters in the picture. Write a narrative about the picture from this character's point of view, telling what happened, who was involved, the result of the actions.

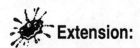 **Extension:**

If possible, pair students from your class with students from junior high school or high school and have them write a story about or for each other. Older students can spend a class period with the children, then write and illustrate a story for them. To follow up, they can return to the classroom to read and present these stories to the younger children. With the assistance of their teacher, children can prepare a story and picture for the older students. This is an excellent learning experience for both groups (and their teachers!).

Autobiographical Writing

 **Objective:**

• To write an autobiography*

 **Focus Activity:**

Display photos of yourself and students on the bulletin board. Relate an early memory; then, ask students to tell something about themselves, including one or two early memories. Show and tell students about some autobiographies (especially some with pictures).

 **Process:**

Discuss why people write stories about themselves. Read portions of an autobiography. Point out to students that stories about themselves are important to others. Discuss important things they might include (names of parents, where they were born, an early memory, events related to them by someone else).

* Prior Planning:

Bring a picture of yourself and have students bring pictures of themselves (baby pictures, if possible). If children do not have baby pictures of themselves, let them use pictures of babies from magazines. If this assignment occurs after school pictures have been taken, students can use a current picture of themselves.

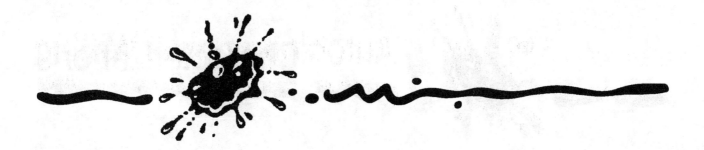

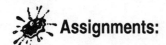 **Assignments:**

Grade K-1

1. Use a current school picture of each student. Student dictates something special about himself/herself. Place picture inside cutout of Christmas tree ornament, star, or other design; place student story beneath cutout. Laminate for gift.

2. Distribute photocopied handouts "This Is Who I Am." (Student Handout 4, p. 95) Teacher or aide can help the child, or the assignment can be completed with parental assistance. Use ideas from this assignment to feature each child on one special day during the year (his/her birthday if possible).

Grades 2-3

1. Same as grades K-1, except students write their own story.

2. Student writes a story about self (offer suggestions based on assignment 2, above).

 **Extensions:**

Have students:

1. Choose just one favorite memory and write about it.

2. Write about their earliest memory, followed by memories at two-year intervals.

3. Write about memories from each summer vacation, special holiday, or school year.

4. Write a series of adventures from their lives that involve riding (e.g., stroller, tricycle, bicycle, skates).

5. Write memories of special people in their lives; telling who they are and giving one special memory about each one.

Characterizations

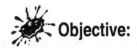**Objective:**

• To understand what characterization means and to write a characterization that shows the physical and mental qualities of a person

**Focus Activity:**

Display pictures of people with different physical characteristics and different emotions; include babies' pictures. Discuss what the picture reveals about the person. Talk about expressions on the babies' faces and have students predict the type of personality the baby will develop.

Process:

Complete one or both:

1. Distribute photocopies of a selected tee-shirt outline. Students create a design that shows their interests and personality.

2. Choose a classroom model, perhaps the child with the nearest birthday. Talk about the child's physical characteristics and personality, always stressing positive points.

©ECS Learning Systems, Inc., San Antonio, Texas

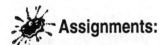 **Assignments:**

Grades K-2

1. Choose someone all the children know (music or art teacher, nurse, principal).

2. Brainstorm with students and list the person's characteristics on the board under categories such as appearance, personality, and type of job.

3. Develop a classroom characterization of the person.

4. Have each child draw a picture of the subject. Invite subject to the classroom and present him/her with children's pictures and the characterization.

Grade 3

1. Follow steps 1-2 of the K-2 assignment above. Students work in groups to develop the characterization.

2. Each student chooses a special person and writes a characterization of that person. Include physical and personality characteristics of the selected person. (This would make a nice gift.)

 **Extensions:**

Grade 3

1. While reading a book (individually or as a class), students develop a "cast of characters" chart for the primary 2 or 3 characters.

2. As the story progresses, students fill in information about the characters' physical and personality traits.

3. Have each student imagine (s)he is one of the characters.

4. Have each student write a first-person story telling what (s)he was like at the beginning of the book, how (s)he changed throughout the story (including what caused the changes), and what (s)he was like at the end of the book.

notes

A Closer Look
at Poetry

Poetry Writing

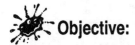

Objective:

• To develop an understanding of poetry and to see poems written and displayed*

Grades K-1: Students dictate poems; teacher writes them. Students illustrate poems and design cover for poetry booklet.

Grades 2-3: Students write and illustrate poems and design a cover for poetry booklet.

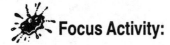

Focus Activity:

Have a student recite the poem "Roses Are Red." Ask students to recall other versions they have heard. Have students share rhymes (jump rope rhyme, folk rhymes).

Process:

1. Read a favorite poem and discuss its meaning (vary according to age level). Talk about rhyming and non-rhyming poems.

2. Model types of poems, adjusting for grade level. Include formula poems and examples of poetic devices such as alliteration and onomatopoeia. Grades K-1 students enjoy simple couplet rhymes.

* The assignments in this section are adaptable to different grade and ability levels. Students in grades K-3 may not be able to write all types of poems; however, the definitions and examples are useful for teacher reference.

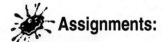 **Assignments:**

Materials

Grades K-1

Distribute photocopied handouts:

- pattern for leaf for the Poet Tree
- pattern for stepping stones
- patterns for various animals
- art materials for illustrations and cover design

Grades 2-3

Same as grades K-1, add:

- nature pictures
- landscape pictures (mountains, valleys, meadows)
- pictures of vehicles

Suggestions for displaying students' poems:

Poet Tree: Decorate a bulletin board to look like a tree with branches. Each student writes his/her haiku or cinquain on the outline of a leaf. These "leaves" become leaves on the branches of the tree.

Stepping Stones: Students write poems (any type) on the outline of a stepping stone. Then, arrange "stones" so they lead to or across a brook sketched on the bulletin board. These can be placed on a student's growth chart. Students write poems on stepping stones to represent memories at different age levels.

Pet Store: Students write poems about their pets on the handout picturing the corresponding animal. Place these poems in a "pet store" sketched on the bulletin board or hang on the walls of a cardboard pet store.

Poetry Notebook

**Assignment:**

Create a colorful, illustrated poetry notebook.

Distribute poetry forms (Student Handout 5, pp. 96-98) and copies of poetry writing (Student Work 2, pp. 105-109). The student handouts for poetry can be used for grade 3 or as a reference guide for introducing various types of poems. The assignments can be adapted for lower grade levels by omitting the more difficult poems and by limiting the number of required poems.

Grades K-1

1. Have a variety of precut designs available (vehicles, animals, flowers, sports symbols).

2. Students select a precut design and cut it out of construction paper to create a cover for their poetry notebooks.

3. On the outside, students place their name, grade level, and date. They may add illustrations.

4. Inside, students can use pictures (drawn freehand, cut from magazines, etc.) to illustrate poems, or they can place their poems on prepared copies of their illustrations.

Grades K-3

Students in grades K-1 will need teacher assistance to complete the following activities.

1. **Cinquain**: Discuss step by step.

2. **Shaped Whimsy**: Use designs such as stars, clouds, school bus. For example, write a rhyme for "Star light, star bright...." on the board. Discuss what students wish for. Have them write their wishes on a star. For a nice bulletin board, write a rhyme on a large star in the center, then place students' stars all around it.

3. **Five-senses Poem**: Students fill in prepared form with one or two words. Example:

Love is....
It sounds like....
It tastes like....
It smells like....
It looks like....
Love makes me feel....

4. **"I Am" Poem**: Students fill in prepared form (Student Handout 4, p. 95). "I Am" poems can be placed on cut-outs of boy/girl and placed on the bulletin board to form a string of paper dolls.

5. **Poem About Someone Else**: Students fill in prepared form. Example:

(Name of person) is.... (color)
(S)he looks like.... (object)
(S)he smells like....
(S)he reminds me of....
(Name) is.... (relative, friend, parent, etc.)

6. **Rhyming Couplet**: Students write simple rhyming couplets about pets or other animals.

Grade 2

1. Follow directions for grades K-1, adding a haiku, name poem (using acrostic format), part-of-speech poem, and free verse poems about nature, landscapes, and vehicles.

2. Students may wish to design their own covers.

Variation: Poems can be just a few words.

3. **Seasonal Poems**: Students complete writing prompts. Example:

Flower or Easter egg design: "Spring is...."
Sun design: "Summer is...."
Leaf design: "Fall is...."
Snow Angel: "Winter is...."

4. **Poem About Emotions**: Students cut out a circle; draw a face with an expression revealing happiness, sadness, anger, fear, etc. Example:

"Love is...."
"Happiness is...."
"Anger is...."
"Fear is...."

Grade 3

Refer to Student Handout 6, p. 99.

notes

notes

Reading and
Writing Connection

Assignments

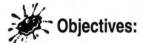 **Objectives:**

• To understand the correlation between reading and writing

• To write a creative discourse that correlates with a book

Students understand and relate to a book better when they draw or write a creative response to it or write their own imaginary story. This section includes brief synopses of a wide variety of books, each with a corresponding writing assignment. It is divided into sections for grades K-1 and grades 2-3.

 **Focus Activities:**

Employ a variety of focus activities to introduce the book:

1. Read the first few paragraphs; ask students what they think the book is about.

2. Look at the cover; discuss what the book might be about based on the pictures on the cover.

3. Read a selected portion about the main character; discuss what might happen to him/her in the book.

Process:

Students or teacher read the book. Discuss one or more components of the book: plot, characterization, setting.

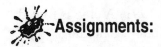 **Assignments:**

An assignment accompanies each synopsis on the following pages.

Grades K-1

Students in grades K-1 can dictate responses to the teacher, have their parents help them for homework, or write their own responses as they are capable.

Beast Feast by Douglas Florian (San Diego, CA: Harcourt Brace, 1994) This book includes 21 original poems about animals. **Assignment:** Draw a picture of your favorite animal. List five words to describe the animal's appearance. Without showing your picture, have the class guess the animal's identity from your descriptive words.

Crafty Chameleon by Mwenye Hadithi (New York: Little, Brown, & Co., 1987) A clever chameleon gets the best of the two bullies, Leopard and Crocodile. **Assignment:** How do you react when bothered by a bully? Have you ever bullied someone else? Answer these two questions in one or two sentences.

Doctor De Soto by William Stieg (New York: Farrar, Straus, & Giroux, 1982) Against his better judgment, a mouse who is a dentist befriends a sly wolf. The wolf eventually wants to eat the mouse. **Assignment:** Describe what you would do if you were the mouse.

Hard To Be Six by Arnold Adoff (New York: Lothop, Lee, & Shephard Books, 1991) A child struggles with being the youngest in his family and enjoying fewer privileges. Grandmother teaches him to be confident and enjoy each moment. **Assignment:** What is the hardest part about being the oldest, youngest, or middle child in your family? If you are the only child, how do you feel about this? Tell the class. Draw a picture that shows your feelings.

A House for Hermit Crab by Eric Carle (Saxonville, MA: Picture Book Studio, 1991) A crab is forced to grow up as he encounters many changes. Instead of being afraid, he sees the future as holding numerous possibilities. This book includes science terms and introduces the audience to a variety of sea urchins. **Assignment**: Draw a picture of your favorite variety of sea urchin found in this book. List five words to describe your animal. (Optional: Write a poem about your favorite sea urchin.)

If You Give a Mouse a Cookie by Laura Joffe Numeroff (New York: HarperCollins, 1985) A child learns the consequences of giving a cookie to an energetic mouse. The book tells how the young host ends up exhausted. **Assignment**: Draw a picture describing your bedtime routine.

I'll Always Love You by Hans Wilhelm (Glendale, CA: Crown Publishers, Inc., 1988) This is the story of a little boy and his wonderful dog Elfie. They grow up together, but one day Elfie begins getting slower and fatter and eventually dies. The boy must learn to deal with the loss. **Assignment**: Write a poem describing the boy's feelings after Elfie dies. (Optional: Draw a picture of your favorite pet and write five words to describe this animal or write a name poem that describes your pet.)

King Bidgood's in the Bathtub by Audrey Wood (San Diego, CA: Harcourt, Brace, Jovanovich, 1985) This is the tale of a king who refuses to leave his bathtub to rule his kingdom. Ideas from the knight, queen, and the court fail. Find out who finally gets the king to leave the tub. **Assignment**: How would you get the king out of the bathtub? List three of your ideas.

Polar Bear, Polar Bear, What Do You Hear? by Bill Martin Jr. and Eric Carle (New York: Henry Holt & Co., 1991) This is a fun audience-participation book for preschoolers and above. **Assignment**: Fill in the blanks at the end of each page. (Allow for class discussion, focusing on the diversity of answers.)

Shy Charles by Rosemary Wells (New York: Dial Books for Young Readers, 1992) Although Charles is a very shy child, his parents realize his value and appreciate his uniqueness. **Assignment**: Class Discussion: Was there something about you that your parents or others either appreciated or wanted to change. How did that make you feel? What finally happened? (Help students design name poems, using acrostic format, describing a personality trait they possess. The class can help, with positive reinforcement, by brainstorming some qualities about each classmate.)

The Grouchy Ladybug by Eric Carle (Wilmington, NC: Thomas Y. Crowell, 1986) Aphids are very small insects. They suck the juice from leaves, and then the leaves die. Ladybugs eat aphids. This is good for trees, shrubs, and other plants. This is a story about a grouchy ladybug who is upset at first because she can't have her own way. She eventually learns a lesson. **Assignment**: Have you ever acted grumpy? Describe how you felt and what helped you cheer up.

The Napping House by Audrey Wood (San Diego, CA: Harcourt, Brace, Jovanovich, 1984) This is the story of a typical nap day at Grandma's, until people and things begin piling on the bed. **Assignment**: Listen to the story up to the last two pages; then write your own ending. (Modify this exercise according to ability. It can be done as a class project or on an individual basis. Compare students' endings with the original.)

The Tub Grandfather by Pam Conrad (New York: HarperCollins, 1989) This story describes the daily activities of the Tub Family and their most recent discovery. **Assignment**: Imagine you are one of the Tub People. Explain which one you would be and why. How would you help Grandfather?

Time Flies by Eric Rohmann (Glendale, CA: Crown Publishers, Inc., 1987) This is a wordless book filled with vivid oil paintings of the Camrasaurus, crested Parasaurolophus, predatory Albertosaris, and flying Pteranedons. **Assignment**: (Students should volunteer for the following assignment.) Tell a story using the pictures in this book. (Record students' stories and write them for the children as a classroom book.)

Grades 2-3

A House for Hermit Crab by Eric Carle (Saxonville, MA: Picture Book Studio, 1991) This is a story about a crab who is forced to grow up as he encounters many changes. Instead of being afraid, he sees the future as holding numerous possibilities. This book includes science terms and introduces the audience to a variety of sea urchins. **Assignment**: Write a paragraph describing how Hermit Crab changes in this story.

Abiyoyo by Pete Seeger (New York: Macmillan, 1985) A little boy who plays the ukulele and his father, a magician, are banished from town. They are left there until the terrible giant, Abiyoyo, appears. The townspeople are terrified. But, the boy and his father come up with a plan to save the town. **Assignment**: Write a speech that the main character might give to his village at the end of this book. Tell what he learned.

Meet Abraham Lincoln by Barbara Cary (New York: Step-Up Biographies Series, 1989) This book includes highlights of Lincoln in his childhood and also later as President of the United States during the Civil War. **Assignment**: Answer the following questions: What made Abraham Lincoln famous? Why did he want to be president? How did he make the world a better place?

Beast Feast by Douglas Florian (San Diego, CA: Harcourt Brace, 1994) A book of twenty-one original poems about animals. **Assignment**: Write a poem about your favorite animal. This can be a name poem or a free verse poem.

Crafty Chameleon by Mwenye Hadithi (New York: Little, Brown, & Co., 1987) A clever chameleon gets the best of two bullies, Leopard and Crocodile. **Assignment**: 1. Explain the meaning of the statement "For brains are often better than strength or size." 2. Explain how you react when bothered by a bully.

Dinosaur Dream by Dennis Nolan (New York: Macmillan, 1990) Wilbur is reading his favorite dinosaur book when he hears tapping at the window. He looks out and sees a baby dinosaur. Wilbur names the little fellow Gideon, after Gideon Mantell, who discovered the first dinosaur fossil. Wilbur realizes he can not keep the dinosaur, so the two journey back to the Jurassic period. This is an adventure Wilbur never forgets. **Assignment**: 1. Compare Wilbur to yourself. Explain similarities and differences. 2. Would Wilbur have been a good neighbor to have? Explain your answer.

Fox Under First Base by Jim Latimer (New York: Charles Scribner's Sons, 1991) Fox has stolen 100 baseballs during games. He tunnels beneath the ballpark and makes a home under first base. Detective Chief Inspector Porcupine is assigned to track down the thief. She needs the help of Fox's new friend Bear, but first she must make Bear understand this mysterious game.
Assignment: Pretend you are Detective Chief Inspector Porcupine. Explain what you would do.

Helen Keller by Stewart and Polly Anne Graff (New York: Dell Yearling Books, 1980) This is the story of Helen Keller. At six years old, she is like a wild, frightened animal. She can not see, hear, or speak. Then Anne Sullivan comes to stay. She traces letters, then words in Helen's hand until Helen understands this will be her way of communicating with others. Helen grows up and dedicates herself to helping others by teaching them what she learned from her teacher, Anne Sullivan.
Assignment: Draw pictures (possibly 4 or 5) that show events in the book. Put the pictures in order and write two sentences under each picture to explain what happened.

I'd Choose You by John Trent, Ph.D. (Irving, TX: Word Kids, 1994) It was the worst day of Norbert the Elephant's life. He had to sit all alone on the way to school. His lunch had been ruined when Heidi the Hippo fell into his mashed potatoes. No one picked him for the ball team. It was a rotten day, and he felt awful! **Assignment**: Write a poem explaining how Norbert felt. This can be a five-senses poem or a free-verse poem. [After students have completed the assignment, read Judith Viorst's *Alexander and the Terrible, Horrible, No Good, Very Bad Day* (New York: Aladdin Books, Macmillan, 1987). Use this at a different time with the following writing assignment: Write a story about your day. Make a timesheet for this day.]

Insects Are My Life by Megan McDonald (New York: Orchard, 1995) Amanda Frankenstein is a bug's best friend. She always steps around spider webs. She hides the fly swatter and clicks her tongue at bats to confuse them and keep them from eating insects. **Assignment**: Do you have a special interest which other friends or family do not share? Write a paragraph describing this interest.

Kermit the Hermit by Bill Peet (Boston, MA: Houghton Mifflin, 1980) This is a rhyming story about Kermit. He is not truly a hermit crab but he is, indeed, a hermit. This bad-tempered, selfish, old crab lives alone in a cave. One day his greedy ways lead him to near disaster, but a small boy intervenes.
Assignment: Write an original ending to this story.

Mirette on the High Wire by Emily Arnold McCully (New York: G.P. Putnam's Sons, 1992) One day a mysterious stranger, who keeps to himself, arrives at the boarding house of the widow, Gateau. Mirette, the widow's daughter, discovers him crossing the courtyard on a wire. She begs him to teach her how he does it. Mirette doesn't know this stranger was once the Great Bellini, the master wire walker. He now has a terrible fear of the wire. It is Mirette who must teach him to have courage again. **Assignments**: 1. Describe a scary experience. Explain how you overcame it. 2. Have you ever helped someone else overcome a fear? Explain. 3. How does Mirette learn to master wire walking? Write a description of Mirette.

Miss Nelson Has a Field Day by Harry Allard (Boston, MA: Houghton Mifflin, 1985) A failing football team finds a new and mysterious coach who gets them into shape and leads them to greatness. **Assignment**: Have you ever been on a losing team? Describe the benefits of losing and winning and how you have reacted to both.

Phoebe the Spy by Judith Berry Griffin (New York: Scholastic, Inc., 1979) In 1776, the year Phoebe Fraunces is 13 years old, her father, Samuel Fraunces, gives her a very dangerous job. She is going to be a spy. During this time, most of the black people in New York are slaves. But Phoebe's father owns a tavern, and their family is free. Her important job is to protect General George Washington (who later becomes President of the United States). **Assignment**: Write a speech that Phoebe might give describing the events of this book. What dangers did she encounter? What did she learn? How did she change? Would she do it again?

Pocahantas by Carol Greene (Chicago, IL: Children's Press, 1988) Pocahantas was the daughter of an Indian chief. She was born around 1596 and died in 1617. She did many brave things, and this is her story, including how she saved John Smith from death at the hands of her father. **Assignment**: Compare yourself with the main character in this story. Explain similarities and differences.

The Biggest Bear by Lynd Ward (Boston, MA: Houghton Mifflin, 1952) Johnny has the biggest bear in the valley, and the bear is still growing. He becomes an inconvenience to the community, and Johnny is forced to get rid of him. **Assignment**: Identify a specific problem that Johnny has and explain how he solves it.

The Jester Has Lost His Jingle by David Saltzman (Palos Verdes Est.: Jester Co., Inc., 1995) A jester loses his job at the palace and enters a troubled world to find laughter. His long journey teaches him that joy is found within. **Assignment:** Pretend you are the jester. Write a story about your life.

The Lotus Seed by Sherry Garland (San Diego, CA: Harcourt Brace, 1993) A Vietnamese family is forced to flee from their homeland to escape a devastating civil war. These refugees have adapted to a different way of life in a new country without losing touch with their cultural heritage. On the night that the Emperor loses his Golden Dragon Throne, Grandmother, then a young girl, sneaks down to the royal gardens and takes a Lotus pod from near the River of Perfumes. She later gives each of her grandchildren a seed from this pod. Grandmother states, "It is the flower of life and hope; no matter how ugly the mud or how long the seed lies dormant, the bloom will be beautiful. It is the flower of my country." **Assignment:** Have you ever been given something special by an older relative or friend? What did this mean to you? How did you respond? Write a story that answers these questions.

The Rag Coat by Lauren Mills (New York: Little, Brown, & Co., 1991) Minna comes from a poor coal mining family. They live deep within the mountains. Her father becomes ill and eventually dies. Minna wants to go to school, but she can't go unless she has a coat. The quilting mothers decide to chip in some of their scraps and make Minna a coat. Minna is thrilled beyond belief, but she is unprepared for the reaction of her classmates. **Assignments:** 1. Have you ever treated someone unfairly because of his/her appearance? Describe the situation and explain ways you could have acted differently. 2. Have you ever been treated unfairly because of your appearance? Describe how you felt and what you or another person could have done to make the situation better. Tell what you learned from this.

Little Sure Shot: The Story of Annie Oakley by Stephanie Spinner (New York: Random House, 1993) One hundred years ago, little girls were supposed to be gentle and quiet. But Annie was one of the greatest sharp shooters in the west, and she became famous all over the world. She could shoot an apple off her dog's head and a dime out of someone's hand. She could even shoot while bending over backward. **Assignment:** Write a paragraph explaining how Annie Oakley felt at the beginning, the middle, and the end of the story. Explain the circumstances that caused these feelings.

The True Story of the Three Little Pigs by Jon Scieszka (New York: Viking Penguin, 1989) The wolf finally gets his chance to tell his side of the story. He claims to have been framed and states that he was only trying to borrow a cup of sugar to bake a cake for his dear, sweet grandmother during the alleged events. Read it and you decide. **Assignment:** Tell a different side of the story about the three little pigs.

Tomorrow Is a Brand New Day by Debby Boone and Gabriel Ferrer (Eugene, OR: Harvest House, 1989) This is a book of poems relating to emotions and childhood issues. **Assignment:** Choose an emotion you experienced this week. Write a poem of your choice, telling how you felt and responded to others that day.

When Bluebell Sang by Ernst Lisa Campbell (New York: Macmillan, 1992) Bluebell is an unlikely star, a little chunky and unsteady in heels. But, this singing cow is talent agent Big Eddie's dream. He doesn't plan to lose his treasure. With the help of Farmer Swenson, Bluebell must plot her escape. **Assignment:** How are Big Eddie and Farmer Swenson alike, and how are they different? When choosing a friend, what kind of person do you look for? Explain your answer in three paragraphs.

Books to Read Aloud

Ramona the Pest by Beverly Cleary (New York: Dell Publishing, 1982)

Hank the Cowdog (a series) by John Erickson (Houston, TX: Gulf Publishing)

Miracle at Clement's Pond by Patricia Pendergraft (New York: Putnam, 1987)

The Trouble with Secrets by Karen Johnson (Seattle, WA: Parenting Press, 1986)

The Legend of the Bluebonnet by Tomie de Paola (New York: Putnam, 1983)

Little House on the Prairie (a series) by Laura Ingalls Wilder (New York: HarperCollins Child Books, 1971-1973)

Amazing Grace by Mary Hoffman (New York: Dial Books, 1991) The characters in many Dial Books display high moral standards.

Madeline at Cooking School (a series) by Ludwig Bemelamans (New York: Division of Penguin Books, 1958) This series is found in Viking Child Books and Puffin Books; both are divisions of Penguin Books.

Stellaluna by Janelle Cannon (New York: Harcourt Brace, 1992)

New American Girl Books

These books are from the American Girls Collection (Middleton, WI: Pleasant Co.). Students of all ages enjoy hearing these books read.

Meet Felicity
Meet Kirstin
Meet Addy
Meet Molly
Meet Samantha

Movies with Character Building Emphasis

Babe—caring
Heidi—empathy and loyalty
The Secret Garden—self-reliance
Apollo 13—teamwork
A Little Princess—courage
American Panda—responsibility
The Indian in the Cupboard—responsibility

Additional Assignments

Adapt according to grade level.

1. After reading a book about a mode of transportation, pretend you are a … (tractor, train, airplane). Write a story about your life in this role. This idea could also work with other inventions or animals.

2. Copy sentences from a book that made you feel … (sad, lonely, happy, fearful, excited, angry). Now write your own sentences that make someone else feel the same way.

3. Make a timeline to fit a particular book. Identify important events from the book on the timeline.

4. Write a short sequel to a book.

5. Make a collage or scrapbook of pictures that relate to a book. Include original pictures and pictures from magazines or newspapers. If you make a scrapbook, put a caption under each picture that explains how it relates to the book.

6. Create a poem about a book.

7. Write a "reader response" to a book in your journal.

8. Rewrite a story; change the personality of a character and/or add a new character.

Book Report and Story Summary Ideas

Teachers of K-2 students will find these ideas useful to summarize or enhance a book through discussion and/or a class report. Students in grade 3 can complete several of the assignments on their own.

1. Choose a character from the book. Compare/contrast this character with someone you know.

2. Describe the setting and tell how it is alike/different from where you live.

3. Rewrite one of the following in your own words:

   • the funniest incident
   • the most exciting or thrilling incident
   • the saddest incident
   • the scariest incident
   • the strangest or most unusual incident

4. Write your book report on a design that represents the book; for example, a report on *The Incredible Journey* (New York: Bantam Books, Inc., 1977) could be written on the sketch of a cat or dog.

5. List the main characters, and write one descriptive sentence about each one.

6. Write diary entries the main character might have written during important times.

notes

Short Assignments

Word Studies

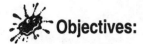

Objectives:

• To understand that figures of speech appear to say one thing but mean another

• To use figures of speech correctly

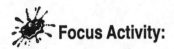

Focus Activity:

Prepare pictures that illustrate figures of speech, such as "It's raining cats and dogs." Discuss what the words *say* and what they *mean*.

Process:

List figures of speech. Students recall those they have heard; teacher adds others.

©ECS Learning Systems, Inc., San Antonio, Texas

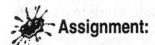 **Assignment:**

Figures of Speech

Students select a figure of speech to use in a sentence. (Grades K-1, students illustrate.) Write what it seems to mean and what it really means; illustrate. Examples:

- We're in hot water.
- He had cold feet.
- Cat got your tongue?
- He's in the doghouse.
- My heart sank.
- Go jump in the lake.
- He put his foot in his mouth.
- Time flies.
- She let the cat out of the bag.

 **Extension:**

Simile Word Study

This is a good way to introduce or emphasize the *simile*. Examples:

- The ground is as dry as a bone.
- I feel as fat as a pig.
- The rock is as smooth as glass.
- We are as busy as bees.
- Her eyes look like stars.
- My little brother is like a tornado.

Students can work independently or with the aid of the teacher to add one or more words to complete the following statements.

- She waddled like a....
- The crash was as loud as....
- My friend is as strong as....
- It is as dark as....
- The baby is as quiet as a....
- I'm as cold as....
- My room looks like a....
- Jumping on a pogo stick makes me feel like a....
- Grandmothers are like....

Additional Short Assignments

All assignments can be used with grade 3 students; adapt for grades K-2.

1. Students remove shoes, trace one foot on construction paper, and cut out the design. On the design, write a story beginning: "Some day I will be...." Place the stories on the bulletin board with the title "Steps to the Future."

   Other ideas for stories include "A Day in the Life of My (or a famous person's) Foot" and "Places My Foot Shouldn't Have Gone." This also works well with hand designs. Beginning lines: "My hand reaches for...."; "One good thing about a hand is...."; "Helping hands...."

2. Using an opaque projector, create a profile of each student. The story on the back should be titled, "All About Me." This makes a good gift for parents.

3. Begin a story with "I am like an ant (or other insect)." Tell why; illustrate your story.

4. Pretend you are your pet or a pet you would like to have. Write a story about a day in your life.

©ECS Learning Systems, Inc., San Antonio, Texas

5. What do you think the statement "curiosity killed the cat" means? Tell about a time you were really curious about something. What happened because of this curiosity?

6. Write a story about "My First … (piano recital, dance recital, tee-ball game, ride on a roller coaster)." Illustrate.

7. On a circle cut-out, draw a happy or sad face. On the other side, write a story about why the face is happy or sad.

8. List creatures that have wings. Choose one and write a story about flying away. Illustrate.

9. Pretend you live inside your school desk or under your bed. Write about your experiences.

10. Pretend you are a flower. Write about the people who come by and how they treat you. Illustrate.

11. Design personal stationery, and write a letter to someone.

12. Choose a picture from the picture file and write a story that tells what happened before and after the picture was taken.

13. Imagine you are a balloon. Tell about the day you fly away. Where would you go? What do you see? How does the day end?

14. Write a story based on a nursery rhyme ("Mary Had a Little Lamb," "Little Bo Peep," "Jack and Jill").

Student Handouts

Peer Response Groups

Evaluation Sheet

Title _____

Author _____

Group Members _____

_____

_____

1. We like the paper because _____

_____

2. Our favorite part is the (place smiling face or check mark)

   beginning   middle   end

   _____   _____   _____

3. Some of the best words are _____

_____

4. Some words we don't understand are _____

_____

5. We would like the story better if _____

_____

Peer Response Groups

Student Handout 2
for Page 33

Evaluation Sheet

Date _____

Title of Paper _____

Strong Points _____

_____

Places needing corrections are (sentence structure, spelling, punctuation, word choice) _____

_____

_____

The thing I like best about the paper is _____

_____

Descriptive words I especially like are _____

_____

I don't understand _____

_____

Expository Writing

Planning Worksheet

A. Name of project _____

B. List the things you need.

_____

_____

C. List (in order) the steps you should follow. You may need more or less than 5.

1. _____

2. _____

3. _____

4. _____

5. _____

D. List any problems you think you might have.

1. _____

2. _____

3. _____

E. How will you correct the problems?

1. _____

2. _____

3. _____

©ECS Learning Systems, Inc., San Antonio, Texas

Autobiographical Writing

Student Handout 4
for Pages 59 & 67

"This Is Who I Am"

My name is....

I was named this because....

My birthday is....

My friends think I am....

My teacher thinks I am....

My parents think I am....

I think I am....

One thing I like about school is....

One thing I do well in school is....

One thing I want to do better is....

I like to help other people by....

Sometimes I need help to....

My favorite food is....

My favorite sport is ....

One thing I don't like to do is....

If I could be in charge of the world for one day, I would....

I wish I could....

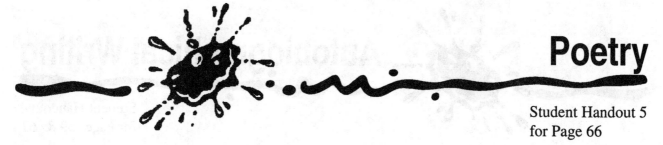

Poetry Forms

Formula poems follow a set pattern.

Haiku: The haiku is a Japanese poem in three lines of 5, 7, and 5 syllables; it can be about a variety of subjects. It creates a picture and makes the reader feel emotion, such as joy or sadness.

Cinquain: The cinquain consists of five lines.

Line 1: one word (noun) to give the title
Line 2: two words to describe the title
Line 3: three words to express action concerning the title
Line 4: four words to express feeling(s) about the title
Line 5: one word that is a synonym for the title

Lanterne: The Japanese have several forms of poetry based on the arrangement of syllables. One of these forms, the Lanterne, is 5 lines long with a pattern of 1-2-3-4-1 syllables. It is often arranged in the form of a Japanese lantern; therefore, it is called the Lanterne.

Diamente: The diamente is a seven-line contrast poem that is set up to appear in a diamond shape on paper.

Line 1: one word (a noun, the subject)
Line 2: two words (adjectives describing line 1)
Line 3: three words ("ing" or "ed" words that relate to line 1)
Line 4: four words (first two nouns relate to line 1; second two nouns relate to line 7)
Line 5: three words ("ing" or "ed" words that relate to line 7)
Line 6: two words (adjectives describing line 7)
Line 7: one word (noun that is the opposite of line 1)

Contrast in thought occurs in line 4. Most people find it easier to start with lines 1 and 7.

Metaphor/Simile: A *metaphor* is a comparison between two things which does not use "like" or "as" but rather takes the form of a direct statement. Example: Anger is a raging fire. A *simile* is a comparison between two things; they are linked with "like" or "as." Example: Happiness is like a strawberry ice cream cone.

Metaphor/Simile Poem: The *metaphor* poem and the *simile* poem follow the same pattern. Note the difference in the last line.

Line 1: noun (also the title)
Lines 2-4: something about the subject (Each line should describe the subject in a different way.)
Line 5: a *metaphor* that begins with the noun from line 1
Line 5: a *simile* that begins with the noun from line 1 and includes "like" or "as"

Limerick: A limerick is a five-line nonsense poem, written in anapestic lines. An anapest is a metrical foot of three syllables, with two unaccented syllables followed by an accented one. The first, second, and fifth lines rhyme and consist of three feet. The third and fourth lines rhyme and consist of two feet. You can allow your imagination to run wild and even create your own words!

Shaped Whimsy: The shaped Whimsy is an imaginative form of poetry. In this form, the poem is printed within a certain shape or in a certain design which reflects the subject of the poem. For example, the shape of a cloud might contain a poem about a cloudy day. Keep the shape simple.

Part-of-Speech Poem

Line 1: article (a, an, the) + noun
Line 2: adjective + conjunction + adjective
Line 3: verb + conjunction + verb
Line 4: adverb
Line 5: noun relating to the noun in the first line

Five-Senses Poem: This poem, which deals with an emotion, is developed by using the five senses. Choose an emotion such as happiness, sadness, love, hate, etc.

Line 1: color of the emotion
Line 2: sound of the emotion
Line 3: taste of the emotion
Line 4: smell of the emotion
Line 5: sight (what the emotion looks like)
Line 6: feeling evoked by the emotion

"I Am" Poem

Line 1: My name is....
Line 2: I am.... (3 words that describe you)
Line 3: I like.... (2 things such as food or sports)
Line 4: I can.... (2 things you feel you do well such as playing the piano, playing ball, etc.)
Lines 5-7: I wish I could (a) go.... (b) change.... (c) learn....
Line 8: Someday I will be....

Poem About Someone Else

Title
Line 1: (Name of person) is.... (color)
Line 2: (S/he) feels like.... (touch)
Line 3: (S/he) smells like....
Line 4: (S/he) reminds me of.... (story, song)
Line 5: (Name of person) is.... (noun: friend, relative, etc.)

Name Poem: Name poems are written using acrostic format. Use the letters of a name for the first letter of each line. Each line then tells something about the person.

Other Poetic Devices

Alliteration: repeating the initial letter or sound within the line. Key to remember: the word *all*iteration repeats the same letter. Examples: softly shining sea; cute cuddly kittens

Onomatopoeia: using words with sounds that tell their meaning. Examples: snakes *hiss*; bees *buzz*, cymbals *clang*; birds *chirp*

Couplet: two lines of verse with rhyming end word

Poetry Notebook

Assignment: Create a colorful, illustrated poetry notebook. It must contain the following sections.

Cover (design as you wish)

1. Original name for your notebook
2. Your name and grade level
3. The date

Specified Poems (Part I): Write an original poem for each of the following types of poetry.

• Haiku
• Cinquain
• Metaphor Poem
• Simile Poem
• Limerick
• Shaped Whimsy
• Name Poem
• Part-of-Speech Poem
• Five-senses Poem
• "I Am" Poem
• Poem About Someone Else
• Rhyming couplet

Specified Poems (Part II): Follow instructions for the following poems. These can be rhyming, free verse, or formula poems.

• Alliteration: 2-line poem using alliteration in first line
• Onomatopoeia: poem using at least 1 or 2 examples of onomatopoeia
• Poem about your favorite person or pet (4 or more lines)
• 4-line poem beginning with one of the following lines:

> Someday I'll be....
> I wish I could go....
> My imaginary friend and I....
> The greatest gift I could give....
> I lost my....
> When I was a baby....

Add as many original poems as you wish. You may write other poems based on the instructions in Section I, as well as free verse poems, or rhyming poems.

Student Work

Assignment:

Dear Parent(s):

We read *Chrysanthemum*, a wonderful book about names, written by Kevin Henkes. The students stamped and graphed their names. Like the character in our book, I want to provide a time for the children to share how they got their names. Please help your child with this assignment. Have your child write his/her name (or trace over your printing of the name) in the first blank provided. On the remaining lines, please print a brief explanation of your choice in naming your child. I plan to use students' completed assignments to create a class book.

Thanks, Cindy Grohman*

* Form used with permission of Cindy Grohman, teacher at Carver Elementary School, Georgetown, TX.

©ECS Learning Systems, Inc., San Antonio, Texas

Writing Samples:
(original spelling and punctuation)

Chloe Watson, K, school year 1996-97 (note from teacher, fill in the blanks)

My name is *CHlOe*.

because (filled in by parents) *the unique name seemed to fit her. She looked like a Chloe, not a Micah, Reagan, or any of the several other names we had selected prior to her birth. When we held her after she was born, and said the other names, they did not fit, but Chloe did.*

In her journal, Chloe dictated some things to her teacher. Example: I like the clouds. I like the blue sky. I like my bed. In addition, she drew several pictures and began to write some words.

Seth Watson, grade 1, 1996-97 school year (journal entries)

9/9/96: I was at a fotball game and a man got hrt hey had to lay on a cot.

9/96: (copied) Just as Moses LiFted up the Snake in the desert so the SUN of Man Must be lifted up that everyone who believs in him

8/96: today i plad socor it wos fun today i got to play the game and today I dug a hol with Jordan i got to fit with INdiN

1/9/97: My Name is Seth Alan. Win I grow up ol bey a football playor i will play for texis tech in collig then i will play for the Lions forst then Cowboys and then Dolphins I will play my best.

Hanna Watson, grade 1, 1994-95 school year (journal entries)

9/27/94: (In response to prompt, "If I Had a Pet") Story plus illustration: I had a pet. But I had to giv it a way. It is a grul. Her name is Mady. I love Mady. She is a gud dog. I mis hur Wawa!! I git to see her. I miyet get to get a noo pet. I thec that I will git a rabbit.

12/9/94: Christmas - Meny meny yiurs a go wen Jesus wus born. that is haw we got Christmas. Santa has 9 reindeer. Haing your stocing.

1/3/95: My New Year's Resolutions are to study more. To love more. To red more. To mide more. To stop eteing so much shooger. Pic-up more. I will fold cloes. I'm going to write more.

2/27/95 (describing favorite part of a book): I likr it bee cos on that page Grampy gis in the water and pools them bac to shor.

Grade 2
1995-96 school year (journal entries)

8/23/95: My Moms name is Kim. She is PTA Presudint. She is a good Mom. One uv my sisters is Chloe she likes to play haws. She likes art. I have a nuter siter her name is Emma. We have sumthing we call a wa-wa it is a pasy (Emma's pacifier). My Dad's name is Ed.

4/17/96: My dog is an old dog. he's fat, tall and flufey. His name in Muffey. He lays arond all day long. And does evreything wrong. But, I still love him. He rolls in the dert. And messis up moms new scurt. He chuwes up my homwork. He messis up my bick. But, I still love him. He chuwes up my Dads work papers. He leves fur all arond the house. He dos not run after a mouse. But, I still Love him. Why you ask? cause He is min.

Grade 3
1996-97 school year

10/15/96:   Roses are red,
Volets are blue,
this poem has a new
home with you!

Student Work 2
for Page 66

Haiku

Emma excitedly
Watches for the white pickup
Runs to meet Daddy

Beautiful flowers
Shimmering in the sunlight
Colorful and bright

Cinquain

Alexandra
Tiny, beautiful
Smiles, eats, sleeps
Makes our family happy
Baby

Lanterne

Spring
Flowers
Time to play
Let's have great fun
Warm

Class
Project
Language Arts
A super place
Great

Diamente

Summer
Short, hot
Swimming, playing, reading
Vacation, baseball, hockey, school
Studying, freezing, skiing
Long, cold
Winter

Metaphor/Simile

Joy
Makes me feel happy
Keeps me warm inside
Brings smiles to others
Joy is a day of sunshine. (metaphor)
Joy is like a day of sunshine. (simile)

Limerick

There was once a big rhino named Sue
Who just did not know what she must do.
So when others would play,
She would just run away,
And so now Sue must live in a zoo.

Shaped Whimsy

I'm like a Ball

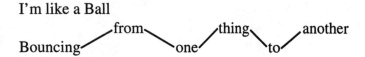

Part-of-Speech Poem

A child
Adorable and beautiful
Growing and learning
Always
Samantha

Five-Senses Poem

Happiness is pink.
It sounds like nuts.
It tastes like candy.
It smells like egg.
It looks like a circle.
Happiness makes me smile. (Jordan Watson, K, dictated)

Anger is as red as a fire engine.
It sounds like chopping a tree down
And tastes as hot as a chili pepper.
It smells like stinky feet
And looks like someone shooting an animal that's becoming extinct.
Anger makes me feel like I want to kick and punch someone. (Hanna Watson, grade 3)

"I Am" Poem

My name is Seth.
I am tough, fast, and smart.
I like football and spaghetti.
I can wrestle and shoot the ball.
I wish I could
go to Disney World;
change problems for sad people;
learn Karate.
Someday I will be a professional football player. (Seth Watson, grade 1, dictated)

Poem About Someone Else

Martha
Martha is soft pink
Like a fluffy blanket.
She is cuddly as a baby rabbit.
And smells like baby powder.
She reminds me of "Lullaby."
Martha is my baby sister.

Name Poem

Cute	**J**oyful
Happy	**O**ccasionally daydreams
Loving	**R**espectful
Observant	**D**arling
Energetic	**A**greeable
	Nearly six

Alliteration

Madison makes magic moments
Playing "Pretend" with her sister
Singing sweetly to her babies
Praying her good night prayers.

Onomatopoeia

The bees buzzed loudly
As the bear searched for honey.
Ouch! Too late now!

Couplets

Humpty Dumpty sat on a wall,
Humpty Dumpty had a great fall.
All the king's horses and all the king's men
Couldn't put Humpty together again.

Free Verse

Hanna Watson (grade 3) wrote the following poem on the computer and printed it in colors, illustrating the thoughts (original spelling).

THE EVERGLADES

I am the Everglades, (dark green)
I have a lot of animals such
as the Blue Haron, (blue)
funny plants like the
Mangrow tree, (light green)
and a lot of marshy dirty
waters that my allagaters swim in. (brown)

About the Authors

Patricia (Pat) Watson earned a Bachelor of Music Education degree from Eastern New Mexico University and acquired graduate hours and further certification at Texas Tech University. During 21 years of teaching, Pat worked at the elementary, junior high, and high school levels. For 10 years, she taught English III, creative writing, and literary genres at Muleshoe High School in Muleshoe, Texas. She was named Muleshoe ISD Teacher of the Year in May, 1993, and Region XVII Secondary Teacher of the Year in August, 1993. Although she retired from classroom teaching in 1994, Pat continues to present workshops and publish instructional material for teachers. Pat has been married to W.T. Watson for 43 years. They have three sons, David, Ed, and Cliff, and 11 grandchildren.

Janet (Nix) Watson graduated from Texas Tech University in 1986 with a Bachelor of Science in Elementary Education. She taught third grade for 3 years in the Longview ISD. During that time, she saw a steady increase in the TAAS (Texas Assessment of Academic Skills Test) scores for her students and attributes much of their improvement to consistent journal writing. Janet and her husband, Cliff, live in Tyler, Texas, where two of their children attend school. A full-time homemaker and mother to Seth, Jordan, Elise, Madison, and Alexandra, Janet plans to return to the classroom some day.